PRESENTED TO

_____

_____

Stories for a Dad's Heart

COMPILED *by* ALICE GRAY
ART *by* MARK KEATHLEY

MULTNOMAH GIFTS™

Multnomah®Publishers *Sisters, Oregon*

STORIES FOR A DAD'S HEART
© 2000, 2002 by Multnomah Publishers, Inc.
published by Multnomah Publishers, Inc.
P.O. Box 1720, Sisters, Oregon 97759

ISBN 1-57673-916-3

Other stories in the Stories for the Heart Collection:
Stories for a Man's Heart
Stories for the Family's Heart

Artwork by Mark Keathley is reproduced with permission from Newmark Publishing USA.

For prints of the artwork, please contact:
Newmark Publishing USA
11700 Commonwealth Drive
Louisville, Kentucky 40299

Designed by Koechel Peterson & Associates, Minneapolis, MN

Multnomah Publishers, Inc., has made every effort to trace the ownership of all poems and
quotes. In the event of a question arising from the use of a poem or quote, we regret any error
made and will be pleased to make the necessary correction in future editions of this book.

Scripture quotation taken from *The Holy Bible*, New International Version © 1973, 1984
by International Bible Society, used by permission of Zondervan Publishing House.

Please see the acknowledgments at the back of the book for
complete attributions for this material.

Printed in China

Multnomah is a trademark of Multnomah Publishers, Inc.,
and is registered in the U.S. Patent and Trademark Office.
The colophone is a trademark of Multnomah Publishers, Inc.

02 03 04 05 06 07 08—10 9 8 7 6 5 4 3 2

www.multnomahgifts.com

Table of Contents

A Gift from My Dad

STEVE DWINNELLS

I have a special box. It's a little, wooden box with two small, shiny handles and a tiny padlock. It's simple— no fancy engravings, no high-gloss finish, no felt-covered bottom. The edges don't fit together well, the hinges on the lid have begun to squeak.

But it's my box, and every now and again I take the small key and unlock the padlock. As I raise the lid, the box releases its special memories, and the memories take me back to another time and another place.

Inside the box are a few knickknacks and a letter. Not much value in the world's eyes, maybe, but a priceless treasure to me. This box was a gift from my dad.

One Christmas Dad made boxes for all three of us boys. He wasn't much of a carpenter. Some of the pieces aren't cut exactly right, and the joints don't fit together well.

But to me, a master carpenter couldn't have made anything better. The box's perfection isn't in its form, but in the motivation behind the making of it.

The box was made by big, calloused hands that knew hard work; by a mind that understood what responsibility means; by a warm heart that loved me. Inside this

box is a handwritten letter addressed to me by my dad. The letter will never be published or nominated for a literary award. It is just a simple letter expressing a tenderness that Dad didn't know how to say very well verbally. It is a note telling me how proud he was of me and that he loved me. In the only way that he knew, he told me that he was glad I was his son.

Dad died a few days after Christmas that year. He didn't leave much money or a big home. But he did leave me that box. With a simple box and a simple message, he left me his love.

As the years have come and gone, the box has taken on even greater value to me as I have come to realize what it really symbolizes. It is a reminder that only the gifts of our hearts hold enduring value.

The smoothly sanded, varnished sides represent the hard work and the perseverance that I ought to strive for. The strength of the wood epitomizes the lasting strength that I need as I struggle through life's difficulties. The

blemishes and the flaws reveal to me that perfection lies not in outward appearances. And like the letter inside, the box shows that warmth and love come from within, from the heart.

Like the box, I have nicks and rough edges, and my joints don't match up well. But just as a letter of fatherly love fills that box, I know that the perfect love of God fills me, making me a masterpiece.

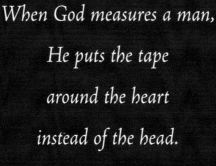

When God measures a man,

He puts the tape

around the heart

instead of the head.

I'm Daddy's Girl

BECKY FREEMAN

One evening not long ago, my husband stayed home with the children while I went to the grocery store. Shopping for a family of six when four of them are males takes a while, so it was late when I got home. When I walked back into the house, all was dark and unusually quiet. After setting down a bag of groceries, I tiptoed into the bedroom, lighted by the soft glow of the moon sifting through the window. Scott was lying there, his hands folded behind his head, staring at the ceiling. He seemed so pensive I immediately thought something was bothering him.

"Hey," I said softly and sat down on the bed beside him. "What's the matter?"

"Aw, I was just thinking about my daughter," he grinned sheepishly. "And how much I love her."

Evidently it had been a very good evening. "What happened with Rachel tonight?" I asked.

"Well," he sighed and searched for words to convey what he was feeling. "I had built a fire outside to burn some excess wood, and the telephone rang. It turned out to be a tough discussion with someone and I was upset. So I went outside to unwind by the fire, and, before long, our little girl came out of the house and snuggled by my side.

"'Dad,' she told me, 'you look like you could use a hug.'" He paused briefly and breathed a contented sigh.

"She's my little sweetheart, you know."

"I know," I smiled as I rubbed the back of my husband's neck. "And I hope she always will be."

The next evening Scott came home from work and found me asleep on the couch. He woke me by tickling my nose with a long-stemmed red rose. Before I could properly gush over it, Rachel strolled in from her room, beaming from ear to ear. Her strawberry-blonde curls

boing-yoinging happily as she plopped down on the sofa beside me. In her small, slender hands she held a lavender basket of fresh daisies and pink carnations. Tucked into the arrangement was a card in Scott's handwriting.

"Thanks for the hug," it read.

Rachel's brown eyes twinkled, and she smiled triumphantly in my direction. "You just got one flower. Daddy gave me a whole basket!"

Love never asks
how much must I do,
but how much can I do.

FREDERICK A. AGAR

Daddy Hands

SUSAN FAHNCKE

I awoke in the night to find my husband, Marty, gently rocking our baby son, Noah. I stood for a moment in the doorway, watching this amazing man with whom I was so blessed to share my life, lovingly stroke Noah's fat pink cheeks in an effort to comfort him. I felt in my heart that something was seriously wrong with Noah. This was one of several nights Noah had been up, burning with a high fever.

Tears filled my eyes as I watched my beautiful husband move Noah's little cheek up against his own chest, so that Noah could feel the vibrations of his voice. Noah is deaf. Learning to comfort him has brought on a whole new way of thinking for us. We relied on our voices, a soothing lullaby, audio toys, and music to comfort our children. But with Noah, we need to use touch, his soft

blankie, sight, the feel of our voices, and most impor-
tantly, the use of sign language to communicate emotions
and a sense of comfort to him.

My husband made the sign for "I love you" with his
hand, and I saw a tear roll down his cheek as he placed
Noah's tiny, weak hand on top of his.

We had taken Noah to the doctor more times than
I can remember. It had been a week and a half and Noah's

fever remained very high and very dangerous, despite everything the doctor or we had tried. I knew in my soul the way only a mother can know that Noah was in trouble.

I gently touched my husband's shoulder and we looked into each other's eyes with the same fear and knowledge that Noah wasn't getting any better. I offered to take over for him, but he shook his head, and once again, I was amazed at this wonderful man who is the father of my children. When many fathers would have gladly handed over the parenting duties for some much-needed sleep, my husband stayed stubbornly and resolutely with our child.

When morning finally came, we called the doctor and were told to bring him in again. We already knew that he would probably put Noah in the hospital. So, we made arrangements for the other children, packed bags for all three of us, and tearfully drove to the doctor's office once again. Our hearts filled with dread, we waited in a small room, different from the usual examining room

we had become used to. Our doctor finally came in, looked Noah over, and told us the news we expected. Noah had to be admitted to the hospital. Now.

The drive to the hospital in a neighboring town seemed surreal. I couldn't focus on anything, couldn't think, couldn't stop crying. My husband reassured me that he felt in his heart that Noah would be okay. We admitted Noah and were taken to his room right away. It was a torturous night, filled with horrible tests that made my son's tiny little voice echo through the halls as he screamed over and over.

I felt as if I were shattering from the inside out. My husband never wavered in his faith. He comforted me and Noah, and everyone who called to check on Noah. He was a rock.

When the first batch of tests were done, the nurse informed us that a spinal tap would be performed soon. Meningitis was suspected. Marty and I had prayer together with Noah. Our hands intertwined, we held our

son and the love of my life lifted his voice to the Lord, telling him how grateful we were for this awesome little spirit with whom he had entrusted us. With tears streaming down his face, he humbly asked the Lord to heal our son. My heart filled with comfort and gratitude.

A short time later, the resident doctor came in. He told us that Noah's first results were back, and that he

had influenza A. No spinal tap was needed! Noah would recover and soon be back to his zesty, tornado little self. And Noah was already standing up in the hospital crib, bouncing like he was on a trampoline. My husband's talk with the Lord was already being answered.

Marty and I grinned at each other through our tears, and waited for Noah to be released from the hospital. Finally, in the middle of the night, our own doctor came in and told us that it was fine to take Noah home. We couldn't pack fast enough!

A few days later, I was cooking dinner. Noah was healing, slowly but surely. I felt at peace and knew my husband was the greatest father I could ever want for my children. I peeked around the corner into the living room and chuckled at the picture I saw. There was my husband, sitting in his "daddy chair," Noah in his lap. They were reading a book, and Marty was taking Noah's teeny hands to help him form the signs for the words in the book. They both looked up and caught me watching

them, and my husband and I simultaneously signed "I love you" to each other, then to Noah. And then Noah put his little arms up, trying to shape his chubby hand in his own effort to sign "I love you" to his daddy. I watched with tears as my husband carefully helped him form his tiny fingers into the sign with his gentle hands. Daddy hands.

There are little eyes upon you,
and they're watching night and day;
There are little ears that quickly
take in every word you say;
There are little hands all eager
to do everything you do,
And a little boy that's dreaming
of the day he'll be like you.

EDGAR GUEST

Of More Value

JERRY JENKINS

A friend, the father of two daughters, admits he doesn't mind putting a little fear into the boys. His daughters may be embarrassed when he asks for a few moments alone with their dates, and he might rather the young men think he's an okay guy than that he's a mean, protective father. But some things are worth a little awkwardness. Boys might think such dads are a little overprotective. To the fathers of daughters, however, there is no such thing as overprotective.

Another friend says he uses a sports car analogy to get his point across. He'll say to the boy, "If I owned the most expensive, exotic sports car on the road and I let you take it for a spin, you'd be careful with it, wouldn't you?"

"Oh, yes, sir, you bet."

"You'd treat it better than if it were your own, wouldn't you?"

"Yes, sir."

"I wouldn't want to think you were screeching the tires, would I?"

"No, sir."

"Well, let me tell you something, just so we're straight with each other, man to man. My daughter is of infinitely more value to me than any car could be. Do you get my drift? She's on loan from me to you for the next few hours,

and I wouldn't want to discover that she was treated with any less care or respect than I would give her. I'm responsible for her. She's mine. I'm entrusting her to you. That trust brooks no second chances. Understand?"

By then, of course, the young man is wondering why he didn't ask someone else out. He's only nodding, unable to speak. Most often, he brings the girl home earlier than promised. The daughter might even complain about her father's approach, but deep down she feels loved and cherished, and you can be sure she'll marry a man who treats her that way.

*In the man whose childhood
has known caresses and kindness,
there is always a fiber of memory
that can be touched to gentle issues.*

GEORGE ELIOT

Kindness

CLARK COTHERN

Ten-year-old Joseph Fisher learned a lesson on kindness when he almost ran over his dad with a tractor. Listen as Joe tells his story.

"I was breaking up some dirt one afternoon while my dad was working on a piece of equipment in the bar ditch on the north side of the field. The old Farmall tractor I was driving had to be turned by pulling a brake on one rear wheel or the other. If you applied the brake to the left wheel, the right wheel kept turning, so naturally, the tractor turned left. If you pulled the right brake, you turned right. It seems so obvious, but when you're ten…you sometimes forget these basic instructions.

"My dad was seated on the opposite side of the ditch, directly in front of where I was headed, and he was intent on his work, so he didn't see the big double

wheels of the tractor until I pulled the wrong brake and started the tractor sliding in the wrong direction.

"I almost panicked, trying to stop the big old thing, but my dad jumped out of the way at the last minute, and the heavy front end of the tractor thumped to a stop right where Dad had been sitting.

"I expected him to come clean my plow (and not on the tractor), so I sat with my hands on the wheel, bracing myself for the explosion. Instead, he calmly walked up to me and asked, 'Are you okay?'

"I couldn't believe it. Here I was sitting on this huge tractor that I had almost steered right over my dad, and he asked if I was okay! When I told him I was fine, he simply said, 'Well, good. Do you know what you did wrong?' I told him, 'Yes, sir,' and he said, 'Great. There's a lesson you won't soon forget.' And he just smiled, patted my knee, and watched me drive the tractor back onto the field. Then he climbed back into the ditch and went back to work."

There are many ways

to measure success;

not the least of which is the way

your child describes you

when talking to a friend.

AUTHOR UNKNOWN

Christmas Day in the Morning

PEARL S. BUCK

He waked suddenly and completely. It was four o'clock, the hour at which his father had always called him to get up and help with the milking. Strange how the habits of his youth clung to him still! Fifty years ago, and his father had been dead for thirty years, and yet he waked at four o'clock in the morning. He had trained himself to turn over and go to sleep, but this morning, because it was Christmas, he did not try to sleep.

He slipped back in time, as he did so easily nowadays. He was fifteen years old and still on his father's farm. He loved his father. He had not known it until one day a few days before Christmas, when he overheard what his father was saying to his mother.

"Mary, I hate to call Rob in the mornings. He's grow-ing so fast, and he needs his sleep. If you could see how

he sleeps when I go in to wake him up! I wish I could manage alone."

"Well, you can't, Adam." His mother's voice was brisk. "Besides, he isn't a child anymore. It's time he took his turn."

"Yes," his father said slowly. "But I sure do hate to wake him."

When he heard those words, something in him woke: his father loved him! He had never thought of it before, taking for granted the tie of their blood. Neither his father nor his mother talked about loving their children—they had no time for such things. There was always so much to do on a farm.

Now that he knew his father loved him, there would be no more loitering in the mornings and having to be called again. He got up after that, stumbling with sleep, and pulled on his clothes, his eyes shut, but he got up.

And then on the night before Christmas, that year when he was fifteen, he lay for a few minutes thinking about the next day. They were poor, and most of the

excitement was in the turkey they had raised themselves and in the mince pies his mother made. His sisters sewed presents and his mother and father always bought something he needed, not only a warm jacket, maybe, but something more, such as a book. And he saved and bought them each something, too.

He wished, that Christmas he was fifteen, he had a better present for his father. As usual, he had gone to the ten-cent store and bought a tie. It had seemed nice enough until he lay thinking the night before Christmas, and then he wished that he had heard his father and mother talking in time for him to save for something better.

He lay on his side, his head supported by his elbow, and looked out of his attic window. The stars were bright, much brighter than he ever remembered them being, and one was so bright he wondered if it were really the star of Bethlehem.

"Dad," he had once asked when he was a little boy, "what is a stable?"

"It's just a barn," his father had replied, "like ours."

Then Jesus had been born in a barn, and to a barn the shepherds and the Wise Men had come, bringing their Christmas gifts!

The thought struck him like a silver dagger. Why should he not give his father a special gift, too, out there in the barn? He could get up early, earlier than four o'clock, and he could creep into the barn and get all the milking done. He'd do it alone, milk and clean up, and then when his father went in to start the milking, he'd see it all done. And he would know who had done it.

At a quarter to three, he got up and put on his clothes. He crept downstairs, careful of the creaky boards, and let himself out. The big star hung lower over the barn roof, a reddish gold. The cows looked at him, sleepy and surprised.

"So, boss," he whispered. They accepted him placidly, and he fetched some hay for each cow and then got the milking pail and the big milk cans.

He had never milked all alone before, but it seemed almost easy. He kept thinking about his father's surprise. His father would come in and call him, saying that he would get things started while Rob was getting dressed. He'd go to the barn, open the door, and then he'd go to get the two big empty milk cans. But they wouldn't be waiting or empty; they'd be standing in the milk house filled.

The task went more easily than he had ever known it to before. Milking for once was not a chore. It was something else, a gift to his father who loved him. He finished, the two milk cans were full, and he covered them

and closed the milk house door carefully, making sure of the latch. He put the stool in its place by the door and hung up the clean milk pail. Then he went out of the barn and barred the door behind him.

Back in his room, he had only a minute to pull off his clothes in the darkness and jump into bed, for he heard his father up. He put the covers over his head to silence his quick breathing. The door opened.

"Rob!" his father called. "We have to get up, son, even if it is Christmas."

"Aw-right," he said sleepily.

"I'll go on out," his father said. "I'll get things started."

The door closed and he lay still, laughing to himself. In just a few minutes his father would know. His dancing heart was ready to jump from his body.

The minutes were endless—ten, fifteen, he did not know how many—and he heard his father's steps again. The door opened and he lay still.

"Rob!"

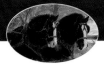

"Yes, Dad—"

His father was laughing, a queer sobbing sort of laugh. "Thought you'd fool me, did you?" His father was standing beside him, pulling away the cover.

"It's for Christmas, Dad!"

He found his father and clutched him in a great hug. He felt his father's arms go around him. It was dark, and they could not see each other's faces.

"Son, I thank you. Nobody ever did a nicer thing—"

"Oh, Dad, I want you to know—I do want to be good!" The words broke from him of their own will. He did not know what to say. His heart was bursting with love.

"Well, I reckon I can go back to bed and sleep," his father said after a moment. "No, hark—the little ones are waked up. Come to think of it, son, I've never seen you children when you first saw the Christmas tree. I was always in the barn. Come on!"

Rob got up and pulled on his clothes again, and they went down to the Christmas tree; and soon the sun

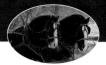

was creeping up where the star had been. Oh, what a Christmas, and how his heart had nearly burst again with shyness and pride as his father told his mother and made the younger children listen about how he, Rob, had gotten up all by himself.

"The best Christmas gift I ever had and I'll remember it, son, every year on Christmas morning, so long as I live."

They both remembered it, and now that his father was dead he remembered it alone: that blessed Christmas dawn when, alone with the cows in the barn, he had made his first gift of true love.

QUIET EXPRESSIONS

He dreams, he plans, he struggles

that we might have the best.

His sacrifice is quiet,

his life is love expressed.

AUTHOR UNKNOWN

365 *Hours*

The greatest gift I ever received
was a gift I got one Christmas
when my dad gave me a small box.
Inside was a note saying,
"Son, this next year
I will give you 365 hours,
an hour every day after dinner."
My dad not only kept his promise,
but every year he renewed it,
and it's the greatest gift
I ever had in my life.

AUTHOR UNKNOWN

What Kids Need

MARTY WILKINS

*T*oday's kids desperately need Dads who ...play catch, enjoy tea parties, or wrestle because the heart of a child is there and they set out to capture it.

...make mistakes but consider them to be wonderful opportunities to learn.

...place an out-of-tune preschool concert or a ten-year-olds' baseball game on life's agenda because they are of infinite worth to those playing.

...listen eye to eye and with both ears even if it means getting on one knee.

...admit when they are wrong and work to make things right.

...model love as action, commitment, and truth even when it hurts because they believe God can work miracles in even the hardest heart.

...love the Lord with all their heart, soul, and mind and know that the rest is just details.

Look, Daddy, I Can Fly!

BECKY FREEMAN

Although I love the slinky, silky gowns my husband gives me every holiday season, this year I asked if he might give me something a little less breezy. I was particularly interested in sleepwear that would wrap warm and snugly around my cold, cold feet.

Thinking it would be a cute joke, Scott gave me a pair of "woman size" pink and white feety pajamas—in a teddy bear print. Christmas evening, I stole away to the bedroom and tried them on just for fun. As I put one foot and then another into the pajama legs, I drifted back to the very first memory I have as a child. I could almost hear my daddy—as he sounded nearly thirty-five years ago—softly singing, "Put your little foot, put your little foot, put your little foot right here..." as I stood on my bed while he helped me into my feety pj's.

My father is one man who has managed, all his life, to keep his child-heart pumping strong.

One rainy spring afternoon, when I was about eleven, I went out to the garage to find my father ascending a ladder into the attic. Though Daddy was sentimental, he was not a handyman, so the sight of the ladder provoked my curiosity. Then he crooked his finger in a silent gesture that I knew meant, "Come along, but be quiet."

I followed him up into the attic and sat down beside him, curious as to the nature of our exploration. But all my dad said was, "Shhh...listen." Then I heard it. The rain, pattering overhead—amplified by our nearness to the rooftop.

"I come up here whenever it rains," Daddy said softly. It was cool and comforting, a tender moment caught—like a snapshot—in my mind.

To my pleasant surprise, my husband turned out to be a rain-on-the-roof kind of guy, too. He even built our bed so that the head of it fits snug against a large picture

window. At night, if the full moon is shining or a soft rain is falling, Scott pulls up the blinds and raises the window and whispers, "Shhh...Becky. Listen." And this, I believe, is part of the reason why the two men I love most in the whole world are my daddy and my husband.

Another amazing thing about Daddy: In all my years, I cannot ever recall my father criticizing me. Not once. Always, he would praise and encourage my efforts—however crazy, however childish.

Not long ago I had a dream; it is a dream I've had for years. In it I can fly. I love these dreams, and while I'm in them, I cannot understand why other people don't just float themselves up to the sky and join me. It is so easy, nothing to it at all. Most of the time I just spread out my arms and take off, but in one of my dreams I piloted a Frisbee. Now that was fun!

But the last dream I had was especially realistic. Once again I was flying, and in my dream I thought to myself, *This is ridiculous. Nobody else is flying except me. I need to find out if this is real or if this is just my imagination.*

So I flew to my parents' home, knocked on the door, and floated up to the ceiling. Then I hovered over my father, who was looking up at me, not at all surprised to find me up there, and I said, "Daddy, listen. You've got to tell me the truth. I really think I'm flying. It feels so real. But I'm worried that this might just all be a dream."

My daddy's answer was swift and sure. "Honey," he said, "it's no dream. You're flying all right."

When I woke up I laughed, but then tears welled in my eyes. How marvelous, I thought, that even in my subconscious, in spite of all logic to the contrary, I have a father who believes I can fly.

For Father's Day last year, I could not find a card that seemed to fit how I felt about Daddy. However, I came across a scene in a children's book that turned out to be perfect. It was a scene with Piglet and Winnie-the-Pooh, walking side by side toward a setting sun. Their short conversation summed up exactly how I felt about my father through the years.

Piglet sidled up to Pooh from behind.

"Pooh!" he whispered.

"Yes, Piglet?"

"Nothing," said Piglet, taking Pooh's paw. "I just wanted to be sure of you."

My dad has been like Pooh to me, his Little Girl-Piglet. Oh, we don't chitchat a whole lot, not like my mother and I anyway. But in every memory involving

my father—from the time he sang, "Put your little foot" as he helped me into my feety pajamas, until this latest dream where he assured me that, yes, I could really fly— my father has been there in the shadows, cheering me on. He has given me the steadfast assurance that always, and forever, I can be sure of him.

SHADES OF LIGHT

Affirming words

from moms and dads

are like light switches.

Speak a word of affirmation

at the right moment in a child's life

and it's like lighting up

a whole roomful of possibilities.

GARY SMALLEY
AND JOHN TRENT

Lessons in Baseball

CHICK MOORMAN

As an eleven-year-old, I was addicted to baseball. I listened to baseball games on the radio. I watched them on TV. The books I read were about baseball. I took baseball cards to church in hopes of trading with other baseball card junkies. My fantasies? All about baseball.

I played baseball whenever and wherever I could. I played organized or sandlot. I played catch with my brother, with my father, with friends. If all else failed, I bounced a rubber ball off the porch stairs, imagining all kinds of wonderful things happening to me and my team.

It was with this attitude that I entered the 1956 Little League season. I was a shortstop. Not good, not bad. Just addicted.

Gordon was not addicted. Nor was he good. He moved into our neighborhood that year and signed up to play baseball. The kindest way of describing Gordon's baseball skills is to say that he didn't have any. He couldn't catch. He couldn't hit. He couldn't throw. He couldn't run. In fact, Gordon was afraid of the ball.

I was relieved when the final selections were made and Gordon was assigned to another team. Everyone had to play at least half of each game, and I couldn't see Gordon improving my team's chances in any way. Too bad for the other team.

After two weeks of practice, Gordon dropped out. My friends on his team laughed when they told me how their coach directed two of the team's better players to walk Gordon into the woods and have a chat with him. "Get lost" was the message that was delivered, and "get lost" was the one that was heard.

Gordon got lost.

That scenario violated my eleven-year-old sense of

justice, so I did what any indignant shortstop would do. I tattled. I told my coach the whole story. I shared the episode in full detail, figuring my coach would complain to the Little League office and have Gordon returned to his original team. Justice and my team's chances of winning would both be served.

I was wrong. My coach decided that Gordon needed to be on a team that wanted him—one that treated him with respect, one that gave everyone a fair chance to contribute according to their ability.

Gordon became my team member.

I wish I could say Gordon got the big hit in the big game with two outs in the final inning, but it didn't happen. I don't think Gordon even hit a foul ball the entire season. Baseballs hit in his direction (right field) went over him, by him, through him, or off him.

It wasn't that Gordon didn't get help. The coach gave him extra batting practice and worked with him on his fielding, all without much improvement.

I'm not sure if Gordon learned anything from my coach that year. I know I did. I learned to bunt without tipping off my intention. I learned to tag up on a fly if there were less than two outs. I learned to make a smoother pivot around second base on a double play.

I learned a lot from my coach that summer, but my most important lessons weren't about baseball. They were about character and integrity. I learned that everyone has worth, whether they can hit .300 or .030. I learned that we all have value, whether we can stop the ball or have to turn and chase it. I learned that doing what is right, fair and honorable is more important than winning or losing.

It felt good to be on that team that year. I'm grateful that man was my coach. I was proud to be his shortstop and his son.

My father never talked to me

about how to treat people.

Every act of kindness

I have ever shown another person

was because I was trying

to imitate him.

PAMELA MCGREW

A Street Vendor Named Contentment

MAX LUCADO

Ahhh…an hour of contentment. A precious moment of peace. A few minutes of relaxation. Each of us has a setting in which contentment pays a visit.

Early in the morning while the coffee is hot and everyone else is asleep.

Late at night as you kiss your six-year-old's sleepy eyes.

In a boat on a lake when memories of a life well-lived are vivid.

In the companionship of a well-worn, dog-eared, even tearstained Bible.

In the arms of a spouse.

At Thanksgiving dinner or sitting near the Christmas tree.

An hour of contentment. An hour when deadlines are forgotten and strivings have ceased....

But unfortunately, in our squirrel cages of schedules, contests, and side-glancing, hours like these are about as common as one-legged monkeys. In our world, contentment is a strange street vendor, roaming, looking for a home, but seldom finding an open door. This old salesman moves slowly from house to house, tapping on windows, knocking on doors, offering his wares: an hour of peace, a smile of acceptance, a sigh of relief. But his goods are seldom taken. We are too busy to be content....

"Not now, thank you. I've too much to do," we say. "Too many marks to be made, too many achievements to be achieved, too many dollars to be saved, too many promotions to be earned. And besides, if I'm content, someone might think I've lost my ambition."

So the street vendor named Contentment moves on.

My list of things was, for the most part, undone. My responsibilities were just as burdensome as ever. Calls to be made. Letters to be written. Checkbooks to be balanced.

But a funny thing happened on the way to the rat race that made me slip into neutral. Just as I got my sleeves rolled up, just as the old engine was starting to purr, just as I was getting up a good head of steam, my infant daughter, Jenna, needed to be held. She had a stomachache. Mom was in the bath so it fell to Daddy to pick her up.

She's three weeks old today. At first I started trying to do things with one hand and hold her with the other. You're smiling. You've tried that too? Just when I realized that it was impossible, I also realized that it was not at all what I was wanting to do.

I sat down and held her tight little tummy against my chest. She began to relax. A big sigh escaped her lungs.

Her whimpers became gurgles. She slid down my chest until her little ear was right on top of my heart. That's when her arms went limp and she fell asleep.

And that's when the street vendor knocked at my door.

Good-bye, schedule. See you later, routine. Come back tomorrow, deadlines…hello, Contentment, come on in.

The heart

of every child

beats to the rhythm

of a father's love.

STEVEN CURLEY

A Father, a Son, and an Answer

BOB GREENE

*P*assing through the Atlanta airport one morning, I caught one of those trains that take travelers from the main terminal to their boarding gates. Free, sterile, and impersonal, the trains run back and forth all day long. Not many people consider them fun, but on this Saturday I heard laughter.

At the front of the first car—looking out the window at the track that lay ahead—were a man and his son. We had just stopped to let off passengers, and the doors were closing again. "Here we go! Hold on to me tight," the father said. The boy, about five years old, made sounds of sheer delight.

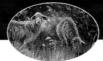

Most people on the train were dressed for business trips or vacations—and the father and son were dressed in clothes that were just about as inexpensive as you can buy.

"Look out there!" the father said to his son. "See that pilot? I bet he's walking to his plane." The son craned his neck to look.

As I got off, I remembered something I'd wanted to buy in the terminal. I was early for my flight, so I decided to go back. I did—and just as I was about to reboard the train for my gate, I saw that the man and his son had returned too. I realized then that they hadn't been heading for a flight, but had just been riding the shuttle.

"You want to go home now?" the father asked.

"I want to ride some more!"

"More?" the father said, mock-exasperated but clearly pleased. "You're not tired?"

"This is fun!" his son said.

"All right," the father replied, and when a door opened we all got on.

There are parents who can afford to send their children to Europe or Disneyland, and the children turn out rotten. There are parents who live in million-dollar houses and give their children cars and swimming pools, yet something goes wrong. Rich and poor, black and white, so much goes wrong so often.

"Where are all these people going, Daddy?" the son asked.

"All over the world," came the reply. The other people in the airport were leaving for distant destinations or arriving at the ends of their journeys. The father and son,

though, were just riding this shuttle together, making it exciting, sharing each other's company.

So many troubles in this country—so many questions about what to do.

The answer is so simple: parents who care enough to spend time, and to pay attention, and try their best. It doesn't cost a cent, yet it is the most valuable thing in the world.

The train picked up speed, and the father pointed something out, and the boy laughed again, and the answer is so simple.

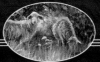

People who really love each other

are the happiest people in the world.

They love their children

and they love their families.

They may have very little...

but they are happy.

MOTHER TERESA

Family Picture

GARY ROSBERG

was sitting in my favorite chair, studying for the final stages of my doctoral degree, when Sarah announced herself in my presence with a question: "Daddy, do you want to see my family picture?"

"Sarah, Daddy's busy. Come back in a little while, honey."

Good move, right? I was busy. A week's worth of work to squeeze into a weekend. You've been there.

Ten minutes later she swept back into the living room. "Daddy, let me show you my picture."

The heat went up around my collar. "Sarah, I said come back later. This is important."

Three minutes later she stormed into the living room, got three inches from my nose, and barked with all the power a five-year-old could muster: "Do you want to see it or don't you?" The assertive Christian woman in training.

"No," I told her, "I don't."

With that she zoomed out of the room and left me alone. And somehow, being alone at that moment wasn't as satisfying as I thought it would be. I felt like a jerk. (Don't agree so loudly.) I went to the front door.

"Sarah," I called, "could you come back inside a minute, please? Daddy would like to see your picture."

She obliged with no recriminations and popped up on my lap.

It was a great picture. She'd even given it a title. Across the top, in her best printing, she had inscribed: "OUR FAMILY BEST."

"Tell me about it," I said.

"Here is Mommy [a stick figure with long yellow curly hair], here is me standing by Mommy [with a

smiley face], here is our dog Katie, and here is Missy [her little sister was a stick figure lying in the street in front of the house, about three times bigger than anyone else]." It was a pretty good insight into how she saw our family.

"I love your picture, honey," I told her. "I'll hang it on the dining room wall, and each night when I come home from work and from class [which was usually around 10 P.M.], I'm going to look at it."

She took me at my word, beamed ear to ear, and went outside to play. I went back to my books. But for some reason I kept reading the same paragraph over and over.

Something was making me uneasy.

Something about Sarah's picture.

Something was missing.

I went to the front door. "Sarah," I called, "could you come back inside a minute, please? I want to look at your picture again, honey."

Sarah crawled back into my lap. I can close my eyes

right now and see the way she looked. Cheeks rosy from playing outside. Pigtails. Strawberry Shortcake tennis shoes. A Cabbage Patch doll named Nellie tucked limply under her arm.

I asked my little girl a question, but I wasn't sure I wanted to hear the answer.

"Honey…there's Mommy, and Sarah, and Missy. Katie the dog is in the picture, and the sun, and the house, and squirrels, and birdies. But Sarah…where is your daddy?"

"You're at the library," she said.

With that simple statement my little princess stopped time for me. Lifting her gently off my lap, I sent her back to play in the spring sunshine. I slumped back in my chair with a swirling head and blood pumping furiously through my heart. Even as I type these words into the computer, I can feel those sensations all over again. It was a frightening moment. The fog lifted from my preoccupied brain for a moment—and suddenly I could see. But what I saw scared me to death. It was like being in a ship and coming out of the fog in time to see a huge, sharp rock knifing through the surf just off the port bow.

Sarah's simple pronouncement—"You're at the library"—got my attention big time.

God has any number of means at His disposal to slice through the haze and mist and get our attention. Are you letting Him get yours?

After He got mine—with my daughter's devastating family portrait—it took a couple of years before I finally

celebrated "being home." It was a banner day for me as the three most important people in my life announced they had a gift for me. I smiled widely...until five-year-old Missy said it was a "drawing of our family." I know this sounds crazy, but my heart started thudding hard in my chest. There it was again, the wide-lined sheet of tablet paper festooned with colorful crayon figures, this time drawn by our youngest. My eyes scanned the family representation. There was Barbara with the yellow hair. There was Sarah. And Missy. And Katie the dog. And a big sun smiling down out of the sky.

And there was a tall guy with a mustache, standing smack in the middle of his family.

Daddy.

I was back in the picture. Back where I belonged. It was time to go out to 31 Flavors and celebrate with some big-time, double-dip cholesterol busters.

Missy's complete family picture still hangs over my desk in my counseling office. Each day as I work with

hurting families needing hope, I keep that little portrait in the corner of my eye. It's a little reminder that I want to be in the picture from now on. But just like you, I have to renew that commitment every time the sun comes up on a new day. It never gets easy, but the payoff is bigger than I could have dreamed.

*The greatest thing in the world
is not so much where we stand
as in what direction we're moving.*

OLIVER WENDELL HOLMES

Look Alikes

LINDA MANGO

REPRINTED WITH PERMISSION OF THE READER'S DIGEST ASSOCIATION, INC.

While working at a medical center, I noticed a distinguished gentleman and his young son on their daily visits to the chemotherapy center. Impeccably tailored suit and a head of lush salt-and-pepper hair made the man stand out. As I admired him and his smiling five-year-old, I found it impossible to tell who was receiving treatment.

One day, as they walked past, my attention was drawn to the boy. The cap he usually wore was missing, and I could now see a shiny bald head. I turned toward the father. To my surprise, he was as bald as his son.

"Look at my dad!" the boy said cheerfully. "He shaved his head so we'd look the same. We're going to grow our hair back together!"

His father simply smiled, looking more distinguished than ever.

Final Season

BOB WELCH

The other night, after the parents had all come to pick up their sons and I was picking up catcher's equipment, bats and, of course, one forgotten mitt, it dawned on me that this was it: the last season I would coach one of my sons' baseball teams.

Two sons. Twelve seasons. Hundreds of games. Maybe three decent umps. And thousands of memories, hidden in my mind like all those foul balls lost in the creek behind the Ascot Park backstop.

Sitting in the rickety bleachers that spring evening—everyone had gone—I found myself lost in thought, mentally walking along the creek, finding those long-forgotten foul balls and listening to the stories they had to tell.

The time our left fielder got locked in a Dairy Queen bathroom during a postgame celebration. The time I

handed a protective cup to our new catcher and he thought it was an oxygen mask. The time a T-baller cleanly fielded a grounder, picked it up and tossed it to his mom, who was sitting behind third base reading *Gone with the Wind.*

For something that became more than a decade-long family affair, it had begun casually enough. While watching one of my five-year-old son's T-ball games in 1985, a manager asked if I would coach second base.

"Uh, second base?"

"Yeah. At this level you need coaches at second base or the kids will forget to take a left and wind up at Safeway."

So I coached second base. And before long, our family's summers revolved around a diamond: me coaching, my wife Sally keeping score, and the boys playing. Like the Israelites trudging out of Egypt, we hauled our equipment, lawn chairs, video cameras and sixty-four-ounce drinks from ball field to ball field, week after week, summer after summer.

The time our right fielder turned up missing during a championship game, only to be found at the snack bar eating licorice and flirting with girls. The time we showed up at an empty field, only to discover that I'd read the schedule wrong and our game was actually ten miles away.

The time I explained to my fifth-grade team that, because we'd given up eighty-nine runs in the last four games, we needed to set a defensive goal.

"It's a six-inning game," I explained. "Let's just try to hold them to twelve runs per game. Two per inning. Can you do that?"

Silence. Then my philosophical right fielder spoke up.

"Coach," he said, "do we have to give up the runs even like that, or could we like give up all twelve in the last inning?"

Our teams were more than a collection of kids. They were extended family, some of whom would end up sleeping overnight and going to church with us. And some of the boys desperately needed that. One year,

of fifteen players, only five had a mother and father living together under the same roof. Once, a boy missed practice because his aunt had been murdered. And I can't count the number of times I took kids home because nobody came to pick them up.

But I've always remembered the advice I heard at a coaching clinic: "Who knows? The six hours a week you spend with a kid might be the only six hours that he actually feels loved."

The out-of-control coach who pushed me off the field. The kid who didn't get picked for my team firing a splat gun at our left fielder. The father who dropped off his son, Willie, and told him to get his own ride home; he and his girlfriend were going to a tavern to throw darts. We went into extra innings that afternoon, and the man's son played the game of his life, going all nine innings at catcher and making the game-winning hit.

We tried to make it more than just baseball. With help from our sons, we established a team newspaper.

A few times I'd put candy in the sack at second base and let players dig in every time they threw out a runner. (Best defensive practice we ever had.)

Sally was our DH—designated healer—with her ever-present cooler of pop and packages of frozen corn for sprained ankles and bruised arms. Once, we had pizza delivered to the ballfield just after we'd lost to a team with one of those scream-and-yell coaches. I think we had more fun that night than the team that won.

The time we won with only eight players. The time Michael, a friend of my youngest son, spent the night at our house and played hours of backyard baseball, the

rules stipulating that you must run the bases backward. The next morning, in a regulation game, Michael hit a hot grounder and promptly took off—for third base.

Over the years we won games, we lost games, and we lost baseballs—zillions of them. But for every ball we lost, we gained a memory. As a family, we laughed together, cried together, got dusty together—as if each of those hundreds of games was a microcosm of real life, which it was.

A weak-hitting kid named Cody stroking a three-run double and later telling his mom, "I'm trying to stop smiling, but I just can't."

My oldest son becoming my assistant coach and reaching a few kids in a way that I could not.

Kids I coached as third-graders now taller than I am.

And, of course, the night we were going to win the city championship. But for the first time in two months, it rained. Instead of playing on a field of dreams with perfectly straight white lines and a public address system,

some official handed us a bunch of medals and called us cochamps.

Later that night, after the postseason pizza banquet, the restaurant manager approached me, broom in hand. "Excuse me, but are you the coach of the Washington Braves?"

"I sure am," I said, figuring he was going to pull me out of my doldrums by congratulating me on the cochampionship.

"Coach," he said, handing me the broom, "your team trashed the indoor playroom. Wanna help sweep?"

Two sons. Twelve seasons. Hundreds of games. As a family, we had shared them all. But what, I wondered, had we missed in the process? What had we given up in order to pursue what some might see as trivia?

Nothing. Because whether your family is together at baseball games or camping trips or rodeos or dog shows or soccer tournaments or swim meets, the common denominator is this: families together—a rarity in our

busy times—making memories. Learning lessons. Sowing seeds that can be nourished only by time.

Regrets? Only one. I wish Willie's father had considered his son more important than a game of darts. He missed seeing his teammates mob him after making the game-winning hit.

The time a tall third baseman was making fun of my 4-foot-9 son at the plate—until my son nearly took off his head with a line-drive double.

My oldest son proudly posing for pictures with his grandparents after the team won a city championship.

The time he played his final game and walking to the

car afterward, it hit me like a line drive in the side of the head. This was it. I'd never coach him in baseball again.

Dusk was descending. It was time to head for home where my family—the boys were now seventeen and fifteen—would be. As I slung the equipment bag over my shoulder and walked down from the stands, I noticed a young father and his son playing catch between short and third.

I smiled slightly and headed for the car, leaving behind plenty of lost balls for others to find.

O Lord...build me a son whose heart will be clear,
whose goal will be high;
a son who will master himself
before he seeks to master other men;
one who will reach into the future,
yet never forget the past.

GENERAL DOUGLAS MACARTHUR

Words for Your Family

GARY SMALLEY AND JOHN TRENT

I'm proud of you.

Way to go!

Bingo—you did it.

Magnificent.

I knew you could do it.

What a good helper.

You're very special to me.

I trust you.

What a treasure.

Hurray for you!

Beautiful work.

You're a real trooper.

Well done.

That's so creative.

You make my day.

You're a joy.

Give me a big hug.

You're such a good listener.

You figured it out.

I love you.

You're so responsible.

You remembered.

You're the best.

You sure tried hard.

I've got to hand it to you.

I couldn't be prouder of you.

You light up my day.

My buttons are popping off.

I'm praying for you.

You're wonderful.

I'm behind you.

The Red Chevy

T. J.

My father loved cars. He tuned them up, rubbed them down, and knew every sound and smell and idiosyncrasy of every car he owned. He was also very picky about who drove his cars. So when I got my driver's license at sixteen, I was a little worried about the responsibility of leaving home in one of his beloved vehicles. He had a beautiful red Chevy pickup, a big white Suburban, and a Mustang convertible with a hot V-8 engine. Every one of them was in prime condition. He also had a short temper and very little patience with carelessness, especially if his kids happened to be the careless ones.

One afternoon he sent me to town in the Chevy truck with the assignment of bringing back a list of things he needed for some odd jobs around the house.

It hadn't been long since I'd gotten my license, so it was still a novelty to be seen driving around, and Dad's red pickup was a good truck to be seen in. I carefully maneuvered my way toward downtown, watching carefully at each light, trying to drive as defensively as he'd always told me to do. The thought of a collision in one of Dad's cars was enough to make me the safest driver in town. I didn't even want to think about it.

I was heading through a green light and was in the middle of a main downtown intersection when an elderly man, who somehow hadn't seen the red light, plowed into the passenger side of the Chevy. I slammed on the brakes, hit a slick spot in the road, and spun into a curb; the pickup rolled over onto its side.

I was dazed at first, and my face was bleeding from a couple of glass cuts, but the seat belt had kept me from serious injury. I was vaguely concerned about the danger of fire, but the engine had died, and before long I heard the sound of sirens. I had just begun to wonder

how much longer I'd be trapped inside when a couple of firemen helped me get out, and soon I was sitting on the curb, my aching head in my hands, my face and shirt dripping with blood.

That's when I got a good look at Dad's red pickup. It was scraped and dented and crushed, and I was surprised that I had walked away from it in one piece. And by then I was sort of wishing I hadn't, because it suddenly dawned on me that I would soon have to face Dad with some very bad news about one of his pride-and-joy cars.

We lived in a small town, and several people who saw the accident knew me. Someone must have called Dad right away, because it wasn't long after I was rescued from the wreck that he came running up to me. I closed my eyes, not wanting to see his face.

"Dad, I'm so sorry—"

"Terry, are you all right?" Dad's voice didn't sound at all like I thought it would. When I looked up, he was on his knees next to me on the curb, his hands gently lifting

my cut face and studying my wounds. "Are you in a lot of pain?"

"I'm okay. I'm really sorry about your truck."

"Forget the truck, Terry. The truck's a piece of machinery. I'm concerned about you, not the truck. Can you get up? Can you walk? I'll drive you to the hospital unless you think you need an ambulance."

I shook my head. "I don't need an ambulance. I'm fine."

Dad carefully put his hands under my arms and lifted me to my feet. I looked up at him uncertainly and was amazed to see that his face was a study in compassion and concern. "Can you make it?" he asked, and his voice sounded scared.

"I'm fine, Dad. Really. Why don't we just go home? I don't need to go to the hospital."

We compromised and went to the family doctor, who cleaned up my wounds, bandaged me, and sent me on my way. I don't recall when the truck got towed, what I did for the rest of that night, or how long I was laid up. All I

know is that for the first time in my life, I understood that my father loved me. I hadn't realized it before, but Dad loved me more than his truck, more than any of his cars, more than I could have possibly imagined.

Since that day we've had our ups and downs, and I've disappointed him enough to make him mad, but one thing remains unchanging. Dad loved me then, he loves me now, and he'll love me for the rest of my life.

How many hopes and fears,
how many ardent wishes
and anxious apprehensions
are twisted together in the threads
that connect the parent with the child.

SAMUEL G. GOODRICH

Driving Lessons

CHARLES SWINDOLL

I remember when I first earned my license to drive. I was about sixteen, as I recall. I'd been driving off and on for three years (scary thought, isn't it?). My father had been with me most of the time during my learning experiences, calmly sitting alongside me in the front seat, giving me tips, helping me know what to do. My mother usually wasn't in on those excursions because she spent more of her time biting her nails (and screaming) than she did advising. My father was a little more easygoing. Loud noises and screeching brakes didn't bother him nearly as much. My grandfather was the best of all. When I would drive his car, I would hit things...*Boom!* He'd say stuff like, "Just keep on going, Bud. I can buy more fenders, but I can't buy more grandsons. You're learning."

What a great old gentleman. After three years of all that nonsense I finally earned my license.

I'll never forget the day I came in, flashed my newly acquired permit, and said, "Dad, look!"

He exclaimed, "Whoa! Look at this. You got your license. Good for you!" Holding the keys to his car, he tossed them in my direction and smiled, "Tell you what, son…you can have the car for two hours, all on your own." Only four words, but how wonderful: "All on your own."

I thanked him, danced out to the garage, opened the car door, and shoved the key into the ignition. My pulse rate must have shot up to 180 as I backed out of the driveway and roared off. While cruising along "all on my own," I began to think wild stuff—like, This car can probably do 100 miles an hour. I could go to Galveston and back twice in two hours if I averaged 100 miles an hour. I can fly down the Gulf freeway and even run a few lights. After all, nobody's here to say, "Don't!" We're talking dangerous, crazy thoughts! But you know what?

I didn't do any of them. I don't believe I drove above the speed limit. In fact, I distinctly remember turning into the driveway early…didn't even stay away the full two hours. Amazing, huh? I had my dad's car all to myself with a full gas tank in a context of total privacy and freedom, but I didn't go crazy. Why? My relationship with my dad and my granddad was so strong that I couldn't, even though I had a license and nobody was in the car to restrain me. Over a period of time there had developed a sense of trust, a deep love relationship.

After tossing me the keys, my dad didn't rush out and tape a sign on the dashboard of the car, "Don't you dare drive beyond the speed limit" or "Cops are all around the city, and they'll catch you, boy, so don't even think about taking a risk." He simply smiled and said, "Here are the keys, son, enjoy it." What a demonstration of grace. And did I ever enjoy it!

The best way

to keep kids at home

is to make the home

a pleasant atmosphere...

and to let the air

out of their tires!

AUTHOR UNKNOWN

Yerr Out!

CLARK COTHERN

My father gave me a great example of self-control when I was a boy watching a church-league softball game.

Dad was forty-three at the time and very active. Though he wasn't known for hitting grand slams, he was good at placing the ball and beating the throw. Singles and doubles were his specialty, and he did the best he could with what he had.

This particular dusty, hot Phoenix evening, Dad poked a good one right over the second baseman's head, and the center fielder flubbed the snag and let the ball bloop between his legs.

My dad saw this as he rounded first base, so he poured on the steam. He was five feet ten inches, 160

pounds, and very fast. He figured that if he sprinted for third and slid, he could beat the throw.

Everyone was cheering as he sent two of his teammates over home plate. The center fielder finally got his feet under him and his fingers around the ball as Dad headed toward third. The throw came as hard and fast as the outfielder could fire it, and Dad started a long slide on that sunbaked infield. Dust flew everywhere.

The ball slammed into the third baseman's glove but on the other side of Dad—the outfield side—away from a clear view by the ump who was still at home plate. Our team's dugout was on the third base side of the diamond, and every one of the players had a clear view of the play.

Dad's foot slammed into third base a solid second before the ball arrived and before the third baseman tagged his leg. But much to the amazement—and then dismay—and then anger—of the team, the umpire, who hesitated slightly before making his call, yelled, "Yerr out!"

Instantly, every member of Dad's team poured onto

the field and started shouting at once—Dad's team-mates were intent on only one purpose: They wanted to win, and by golly they knew they were right!

The two runners who had crossed home plate before Dad was called out had brought the score to within one. If Dad was out—and we all knew he wasn't—his team was robbed of a single run.

With only one inning left, this one bad call could cost them the game.

But just as the fracas threatened to boil over into a miniriot, Dad silenced the crowd. As the dust settled around him, he held up a hand. "Guys, stop!" he yelled. And then more gently, "There's more at stake here than being right. There's something more important here than winning a game. If the ump says I'm out, I'm out."

And with that, he dusted himself off, limped to the bench to get his glove (his leg was bruised from the slide), and walked back into left field all by himself, ready to begin the last inning. One by one, the guys on

his team gave up the argument, picked up their own gloves, and walked out to their positions on the field.

I've got to tell you, I was both bewildered and proud that night. My dad's character was showing, and it sparkled. He may have been dusty, but I saw a diamond standing out there under the lights, a diamond more valuable than all the points his team might have scored.

For a few minutes that evening I was a rich kid, basking in my father's decision to be a man, to hold his tongue instead of wagging it, to settle the dust instead of settling a score. I knew his character at that selfless moment was worth more than all the gold-toned plastic trophies you could buy.

Dad held court that night and the verdict came down hard and he was convicted of being a man...and the evidence that proved it was his powerful use of that awe-inspiring weapon.

Self-control.

*The ultimate measure of a man
is not where he stands
in moments of comfort and convenience,
but where he stands
at times of challenge and controversy.*

MARTIN LUTHER KING, JR.

A Small Boy's Prayer

ROB PARSONS

One night, when my son was small, I was saying prayers with him. The next day I was due to fly abroad to address an international law conference, and I was quite nervous. I've prayed many prayers for him, but this time asked him to pray for me. This is what he said: "Dear Lord, please help my dad to be brave, and not to make too many mistakes." It's not a bad prayer for every father.

"As for me and my household,
we will serve the LORD."

JOSHUA 24:15

A Father's Prayer
of Enlightenment

JOHN ELLIS

Dear heavenly Father, can you forgive me for hurting my children?

I came from a poor background so I thought that a big house would make my children feel important. I didn't realize that all it takes is my love.

I thought money would bring them happiness, but all it did was make them think that things were more important than people.

I thought spanking them would make them tough so that they could defend themselves. All it did was stop me from seeking wisdom so that I could discipline and teach them.

I thought that leaving them alone would make them independent. All it did was force my one son to be the father to my second son.

I thought that by smoothing over all of the family problems I was keeping peace. All I was teaching them was to run rather than lead.

I thought that by pretending to be the perfect family in public that I was bringing them respectability. All I was teaching them was to live a lie and keep the secret.

I thought that all I had to do to be a father was make money, stay at home, and supply all their material needs. All I taught them was that there is more to being a dad. The problem is they will have to guess what being a dad really is.

And dear God,

I hope you can read this prayer. My tears have smudged a lot of words.

The Lord is near to all

that call upon Him; yea,

He can feel breath when no voice

can be heard for faintness.

JOHN TRAPP

Father's Day: A Tribute

MAX LUCADO

Today is Father's Day. A day of cologne. A day of hugs, new neckties, long-distance phone calls, and Hallmark cards.

Today is my first Father's Day without a father. For thirty-one years I had one. I had one of the best. But now he's gone. He's buried under an oak tree in a west Texas cemetery. Even though he's gone, his presence is very near—especially today.

It seems strange that he isn't here. I guess that's because he was never gone. He was always close by. Always available. Always present. His words were nothing novel. His achievements, though admirable, were nothing extraordinary.

But his presence was.

Like a warm fireplace in a large house, he was a source of comfort. Like a sturdy porch swing or a big-branched elm in the backyard, he could always be found…and leaned upon.

During the turbulent years of my adolescence, Dad was one part of my life that was predictable. Girlfriends came and girlfriends went, but Dad was there. Football season turned into baseball season and turned into football season again and Dad was always there. Summer vacation, homecoming dates, algebra, first car, driveway basketball—they all had one thing in common: his presence.

And because he was there life went smoothly. The car always ran, the bills got paid, and the lawn stayed mowed. Because he was there the laughter was fresh and the future was secure. Because he was there my growing up was what God intended growing up to be; a storybook scamper through the magic and mystery of the world.

Because he was there we kids never worried about things like income tax, savings accounts, monthly bills, or mortgages. Those were the things on Daddy's desk.

We have lots of family pictures without him. Not because he wasn't there, but because he was always behind the camera.

He made the decisions, broke up the fights, chuckled at Archie Bunker, read the paper every evening, and fixed breakfast on Sundays. He didn't do anything unusual. He only did what dads are supposed to do—be there.

He taught me how to shave and how to pray. He helped me memorize verses for Sunday school and taught me that wrong should be punished and that right-ness has its own reward. He modeled the importance of getting up early and staying out of debt. His life expressed the elusive balance between ambition and self-acceptance.

He comes to mind often. When I smell Old Spice aftershave, I think of him. When I see a bass boat, I see

his face. And occasionally, not too often, but occasionally when I hear a good joke (the kind Red Skelton would tell), I hear him chuckle. He had a copyright chuckle that always came with a wide grin and arched eyebrows.

Daddy never said a word to me about sex or told me his life story. But I knew that if I ever wanted to know, he would tell me. All I had to do was ask. And I knew if I ever needed him, he'd be there.

Like a warm fireplace.

Maybe that's why this Father's Day is a bit chilly. The fire has gone out. The winds of age swallowed the late splendid flame, leaving only golden embers. But there is a strange thing about those embers, stir them a bit and a flame will dance. It will dance only briefly, but it will dance. And it will knock just enough chill out of the air to remind me that he is still…in a special way, very present.

❧

If you take being a father seriously,
you'll know that you're not big enough
for the job, not by yourself….
Being a father will put you
on your knees if nothing else ever did.

ELISABETH ELLIOT

Acknowledgments

A diligent search has been made to trace original ownership, and when necessary, permission to reprint has been obtained. If I have overlooked giving proper credit to anyone, please accept my apologies. Should any attribution be found to be incorrect, the publisher welcomes written documentation supporting correction for subsequent printings. For material not in the public domain, grateful acknowledgment is given to the publishers and individuals who have granted permission for use of their material.

Acknowledgments are listed by story title in the order they appear in the book. For permission to reprint any of the stories, please request permission from the original source listed below.

"A Gift from My Dad" by Steve Dwinnells from *Decision* magazine, December 1997. (Billy Graham Evangelistic Association, Minneapolis, MN) © 1997 by Steve Dwinnells. Used by permission of the author. All rights reserved.

"I'm Daddy's Girl" by Becky Freeman from *Marriage 911* (Broadman and Holman Publishers, Nashville, TN) © 1996. All rights reserved. Used by permission.

"Daddy Hands" by Susan Fahncke. 1325 North Highway 89, Suite 315F, Farmington, UT 84025. Website: www.2theheart.com, e-mail: susan@FawnKey.com. Used by permission of the author.

"Of More Value" by Jerry B. Jenkins from *Still the One*, published by Focus on the Family. Copyright © 1995 by Jerry B. Jenkins. All right reserved. International Copyright secured. Used by permission.

"Kindness" by Clark Cothern from *At the Heart of Every Great Father*, © 1998. Used by permission of Multnomah Publishers, Sisters, OR.

"Christmas Day in the Morning" by Pearl S. Buck, Harold Ober Associates, © 1955. Used by permission.

"365 Hours," author unknown. Excerpted from *God's Little Devotional Book for Dads*, Honor Books, © 1995.

"What Kids Need" by Marty Wilkins, high school teacher, Milwaukie, OR. Used by permission. Marty is thankful for his wife, Becky, and his sons, Ryan, Taylor, and Caleb.

"Look, Daddy, I Can Fly!" by Becky Freeman from *Still Lickin' the Spoon* (Broadman and Holman Publishers, 1997). All rights reserved. Used by permission.

"Shades of Light" by Gary Smalley and John Trent from *Leaving the Light On* © 1994. Used by permission of Multnomah Publishers, Sisters, OR.

"Lessons in Baseball" by Chick Moorman from *Where the Heart Is: Stories of Home and Family* (Personal Power Press, Merrill, MI), © 1996. Used by permission of the author. For information on his newest book, *Parent Talk: Words that Empower, Words that Wound*, contact him at 1-800-797-4133.

"A Street Vendor Named Contentment" by Max Lucado from *No Wonder They Call Him the Savior*, © 1986. Used by permission of Multnomah Publishers, Sisters, OR.

"A Father, a Son, and an Answer" by Bob Greene. © 1993, Tribune Media Services, Inc. All rights reserved. Reprinted with permission from the May 1995 *Reader's Digest* and Tribune Media Services.

"Family Picture" by Gary Rosberg from *Guard Your Heart*, © 1994. Used by permission of Multnomah Publishers, Sisters, OR.